# DRAMA BIBLE FOR YOUNG PEOPLE

BY

## MARY M. RUSSELL

*Instructor in Young People's Methods, School of Religious Education and Social Service, Boston University and Formerly Associate Superintendent of Young People's Department, Board of Sunday Schools*

NEW YORK
GEORGE H. DORAN COMPANY

COPYRIGHT, 1921,
BY GEORGE H. DORAN COMPANY

PRINTED IN THE UNITED STATES OF AMERICA

TO THE YOUNG PEOPLE
OF
SECOND CONGREGATIONAL CHURCH, BOSTON
WHO FIRST DRAMATIZED MANY OF THESE STORIES

# INTRODUCTION

These dramatizations are arranged for *young people,* those in the teens, and not for children. While the younger boys and girls enjoy dramatizing a story and many teachers in Primary and Junior departments have, in the last few years, made use of dramatization as a means of impressing the lesson, still, this form of presenting a story should not be confined to the lower grades.

The stories given in this book have grown out of actual experience with the adolescent group. The dramatic instinct is very strong during the adolescent years, and should be used as a means of teaching moral and religious truth, and for providing young people the ideals needed.

Many of the dramatizations have been produced by Intermediates and Seniors, having been given at Sunday-Schools as a special feature of the worship service; at prayer meetings, as a Scripture reading; at concerts as a part of the program; at summer camps as a Sunday service. The first of these stories was dramatized because a pastor of a large city church was anxious to interest the young people in the mid-week service and was willing to vary his program to meet their needs. The dramatization was presented as the

## INTRODUCTION

Scripture lesson and the talk of the hour was based on the message of the story.

Not only do dramatizations appeal to the young people but they afford an opportunity for the church to use her young life. Churches are constantly lamenting the absence from the services of the young people. Perhaps if they had more to do in the work of the church their interest and attendance would be correspondingly great. Young people are truly religious, but theirs is not the religion of maturity. It does not express itself naturally in testimony meetings, but in ways which lie within the interests and abilities of youth. Theirs is a religion of action, not speech. Young life craves activity. Idle listener is not the rôle that appeals most strongly to them. At a State Convention of one of the leading denominations, four young men from different sections of the State were asked to speak on the question: "What do the Young People Ask of the Church?" Every one of the four had the same message—"Give us something to do."

Because of their youth they are not elected to office; because of inexperience and custom they do not contribute much to discussions in prayer meetings. They are, however, religious and need opportunity to express themselves. Through the dramatized story the youth finds one way. His attitude toward the story and the characters represented is one of respect and reverence. As he tries to impersonate a strong, noble, loyal character he finds within his own heart a desire to be

## INTRODUCTION

the character he is trying to portray. Many a youth can tell, if he will, of the incentive to achievement and of the finding of an ideal which has come to him as he has helped dramatize a story. Young people are entitled to a place in the local church program. If they can help in some of the services by dramatizing a Bible story the church is wise that provides them with such an opportunity.

The dramatizations given here have been made very simple. The words of the story have been taken, for the most part, directly from the Bible narrative, so that the youth is learning Scripture as well as a story. A good preparation for the dramatization is to call together all who are to have a part in the production, and read or tell them the whole story before the parts are assigned. By this plan each is made familiar with the story and its message before he begins to prepare his own part. Few rehearsals are necessary. The ideal way to dramatize a story is to have no printed parts assigned but to allow each person to select the character he prefers and to interpret the part as it appeals to him. This is the most successful plan for use with children. To follow such a method, story-telling or group study must precede the dramatizations. This is often not feasible or easily arranged for young people, so this book, with its suggestions, is designed to help the busy teacher, director or preacher who is interested in giving the young people a chance to help in a way that is natural and enjoyable.

## INTRODUCTION

Through dramatizing Bible Stories the young people not only are given a part in the church services but they are made more familiar with the stories of the Bible. Interest or curiosity invariably leads the one participating to read the biblical account of the story. Some of the stories cover a number of chapters, and as the youth reads he finds a new interest in the story. Never will he forget a story he has helped to dramatize, or fail to appreciate its teaching. To him, more than to those in the audience, comes the message of the story; to him comes higher ideals, deeper motives, a stronger desire to be and to do, so that the dramatized story becomes but another means of teaching, a further aid in character building.

It will be noticed that some of the dramatizations require only girls, others only boys, while others are for mixed groups, so that selection can be made to fit any group. There are twelve stories, the thought being that once each month, at least, the young people should be allowed to present a story. After a few presentations the young people will often be able to prepare stories of their own choosing and work out the dramatizations for themselves.

MARY M. RUSSELL.

*Boston, Mass.*

# COSTUMES, SCENERY, STAGE PROPERTIES

The costuming is a very simple matter. The oriental garments were loose flowing robes, both for men and women. Capes, shawls, scarfs and strips of bright colored cheese cloth make excellent costumes. Churches having vested choirs are well supplied with gowns which may be used in many cases. College gowns may be borrowed from friends in the neighborhood. Dresses of cheese cloth can be made with little work and expense. Churches which are located in the cities where the mission boards have rooms may often be able to borrow costumes from the board rooms. Usually each person representing a character will be responsible for his own costume. He will, doubtless, need help in planning it. Pictures of oriental scenes will often furnish helpful suggestions.

Screens, draperies and plants can usually be made to provide sufficient scenery. Where a platform or portion of a house is needed it can be easily constructed by some of the older boys. There are often those who can not speak in public who will be glad to have a part in the preparation and to help by building needed scenery. A dark drapery thrown over a box or chair can be made to represent a rock; draperies hung over screens will make a good representation of a city wall.

Palms, ferns and other potted plants can be used very effectively for out-of-door scenes, river banks and fields. Many churches are provided with ferns which can be used; sometimes florists will lend palms and other large plants, and in many churches will be found the friendly merchant who is usually willing to lend his plants and will often deliver them at the church.

Screens may be used in the churches which are not provided with a curtain. Some of the stories, as *Easter Morning* II, do not require a curtain but can be given on any platform and without scenery. The imagination of the young people will enable them to make the story live so that both they and their audience will be able to see the pictures even without much scenery. The aim in presenting the stories is not to give a finished production but to make the message of the story felt. This will be accomplished more by the way the young people interpret the parts assigned to them than by any stage arrangements or scenery.

# CONTENTS

|     |                                                      | PAGE |
|-----|------------------------------------------------------|------|
|     | INTRODUCTION                                         | vii  |
|     | COSTUMES, SCENERY, STAGE PROPERTIES                  | xi   |
| I   | A MOTHER'S FAITH (MOSES)                             | 17   |
| II  | IN QUEST OF A GREAT TREASURE (NAAMAN)                | 22   |
| III | A WOMAN WHO DARED (ESTHER)                           | 29   |
| IV  | THE OUTCOME OF A SECRET (BARTIMEUS)                  | 35   |
| V   | EASTER MORN                                          | 39   |
| VI  | EASTER MORNING                                       | 47   |
| VII | A SEARCH FOR A WIFE (ISAAC AND REBECCA)              | 53   |
| VIII| THE VALUE OF PREPARATION (TEN VIRGINS)               | 59   |
| IX  | THE SECRET OF SUCCESS (NEHEMIAH)                     | 63   |
| X   | A NEIGHBOR AND HIS WORK (GOOD SAMARITAN)             | 74   |
| XI  | A GIRL WHO KNEW HOW TO BE A FRIEND (RUTH)            | 78   |
| XII | A THANKSGIVING SERVICE (MIRIAM)                      | 83   |
| XIII| THE FIRST CHRISTMAS                                  | 88   |

# DRAMATIZED BIBLE STORIES
# FOR YOUNG PEOPLE

# DRAMATIZED BIBLE STORIES FOR YOUNG PEOPLE

## A MOTHER'S FAITH

CHARACTERS:
  Mother.
  Babe.
  Sister.
  Friends.
  Princess.
  Five Maidens.

### SCENE I

PLACE: *Home of Moses' Parents.*

*Mother.* My son has been hidden for three months but now he grows older and concealment is no longer possible. Where can I find for him a place of safety?

*Friend.* I know not. Pharaoh hath said, "Every son that is born of a Hebrew ye shall cast into the river and only daughters shall ye save alive."

*Mother.* My beautiful boy shall not perish. Surely the Lord will show me a way of escape. My trust is in Him. He will not forsake me.

*Friend.* Thou couldst make for thy son a cradle of rushes and hide him in the reeds by the river. There thou couldst watch over him to feed and to care for him, and perchance his hiding place would never be discovered and so his life would be saved.

*Mother.* That will I do! [*Turning to Sister.*] Fetch me the rushes! We will make for him an ark and cover it with slime and pitch and place the child therein and lay the ark in the flags by the river's brink. Thou, his sister, shalt watch from afar, that no evil befall him. The Lord shall be with thee in thy task. Make haste! Bring the rushes.

[*Exit Sister.*

[*Mother bends over the babe as if in prayer.*

*Friend.* [*Approaching mother.*] The Lord hear thee in the day of thy trouble: the name of the God of Jacob defend thee: Send thee help from the sanctuary, and strengthen thee out of Zion; Remember all thy offerings and accept thy burnt sacrifices; Grant thee according to thine own heart's desire and fulfill all thy petitions. We will rejoice in thy salvation, and in the name of our God will we set up our banners; The Lord fulfill all thy petitions. Some trust in chariots and some trust in horses, but we will remember the name of our God. They are brought down and fallen, but we are risen and stand upright. Save, Lord, hear us when we call. [*The women embrace.*

[*Soft music behind scenes.*

CURTAIN

## SCENE II

PLACE: *By the river bank. Palms, etc., to give the effect. Ark among the reeds. Sister hidden near.*

[*Enter Princess and Maidens.*

*First Maiden.* Wilt thou not rest here in the shade, O Princess? Surely thou art wearied with thy long walk by the river side.

*Princess.* I will rest me at thy suggestion, O my friend, and thou shalt sing to me.

[*First Maiden sings. Any pretty nature song that has no modern Christian sentiment.*

*Princess.* What is that yonder that mine eyes behold?

*Second Maiden.* It is, indeed, a strange object to be among the reeds. I go to look upon it that I may tell thee what it is.

*Princess.* Nay, rather bring it to me.

[*Two maidens bring ark to Princess. She peers in.*

*Princess.* A babe! He weeps! Give him to me. He is one of the Hebrew children.

*Fourth maiden.* What shall be done with him?

*Princess.* I shall keep him for my own child.

*Fourth Maiden.* But thy father Pharaoh loveth not the Hebrew children. Has he not commanded that all the male children shall be put to death?

*Princess.* True, nevertheless, I keep the child. Already he doth cause me to love him. He shall be called Moses, because I drew him out of the water.

[*Enter sister.*

*Sister.* If it please thee, O Princess, hear me! Shall I go and call for thee a nurse of the Hebrew women that she may nurse the child for thee?

*Princess.* Yes, that thou shalt do. Go bring the Hebrew nurse. She will know well how to care for the babe. Go quickly!

[*Exit sister.*

*Fifth Maiden.* Fair indeed is his countenance.

*Princess.* He shall be to me a son. As the Princess' son shall he be honored. None shall do him harm.

[*Enter sister and mother.*

*Sister.* Behold, O Princess, a woman of the Hebrews who shall nurse for thee the child.

*Princess.* Dost thou know well how to care for a babe? Wilt thou nurse him for me until the time when I can have him with me at my father's house?

*Mother.* Yes, verily, such care as his mother would give him will I give him. Only let me be his nurse!

*Princess.* Take the child away, nurse it for me, and I will give thee wages. [*Looking at child.*] Thou blessed babe. [*Gives babe to mother.*

*Princess.* [*Rising.*] Let us return. I would not tarry longer.

[*Exeunt all.*

CURTAIN

## SCENE III

PLACE: *Same as in Scene I. Room in semi-darkness. Soft music of violin in distance.*

*Mother seated with child in her arms at center of stage, sister in background. Rising slowly, mother places child on couch and, standing in attitude of prayer, offers the following petition, rising to exaltation at the close.*

*Mother.* While I live, I will praise the Lord! I cried unto God with my voice, even unto God with my voice, and he gave ear unto me. In the day of my trouble, I sought the Lord. In the day when I cried, Thou answered me and strengthened me with strength in my soul. Though I walk in the midst of trouble, Thou wilt revive me for Thy loving kindness and for Thy truth. Cause me to hear Thy loving kindness in the morning for in Thee do I trust. Cause me to know the way in which I should walk for I lift my soul unto Thee. Every day will I bless Thee, and I will extol Thy name forever and ever. Great is the Lord, and greatly to be praised!

[*An appropriate selection played softly on violin during the mother's speech adds much to the impressiveness of the presentation.*]

**CURTAIN**

# IN QUEST OF A GREAT TREASURE

CHARACTERS:
  Naaman, *captain of the host of the king of Syria.*
  Naaman's wife.
  Israelitish maiden, *a captive and servant to Naaman's wife.*
  Elisha, *the prophet of Samaria.*
  Gehazi, *Elisha's servant.*
  Naaman's attendants.
  Servant.

## SCENE I

PLACE: *A room in Naaman's house, wife seated on couch. Israelitish maiden busy making the woman comfortable. Woman appears sad and indifferent.*

*Maiden.* Is there aught else that I can do for thee, my mistress?
*Mistress.* [*Shakes head slowly.*] No, nothing.
*Maiden.* Art thou ill this morning?
*Mistress.* No.
*Maiden.* It grieves me to see my dear mistress so sad. If I could only do something to make her glad. Is there naught that I can do?
*Mistress.* No, oh, no. [*Rises from couch.*] No one can help my sorrow. Oh, Naaman, Naa-

man, my husband! Why should this terrible affliction come upon thee? Thou art not only a great man but thou art a good man, valiant and honorable, and needed by thy king,—and yet, thou must die!

*Maiden.* Die—the master! Is there to be another war? Surely the enemy can not prevail against the mighty Naaman. Hath he not already delivered Syria?

*Mistress.* Ah, no. In war he might have a chance for his life, but not now, not now. Dost thou remember the white spot which appeared on Naaman's hand and which hath troubled him for some time? This day he hath told me that it is the mark of leprosy. Leprosy, that hideous disease, that living death, which makes a man an exile, an object of loathing to all who see him and a burden unto himself. Oh, Naaman, what doth thy glory and honor avail thee now? It would have been better that thou shouldst have fallen in battle. Oh, Naaman, my husband!

*Maiden.* Would God that my lord were with the prophet that is in Samaria for he would recover him of his leprosy!

*Mistress.* What sayest thou? There is no cure for leprosy.

*Maiden.* I know it is said so, but indeed there is a prophet who lives in my country and who hath cured many of this dread disease. If only my lord were there, the prophet could heal him!

*Mistress.* Tell me the name of the prophet! Quick!

*Maiden.* He is called Elisha. Many are the wonderful deeds he hath performed, for he is a prophet of the Lord Jehovah who giveth him marvelous power.

*Mistress.* [*Claps hand; servant enters.*] Go quickly. Call thy master. Bid him come at once. [*Mistress pacing floor.*] Oh, if it is true! [*Exit servant.*] If there be a way of escape from this terrible thing! Why doth not he hasten? [*Enter Naaman.*] Oh, Naaman, Naaman, listen! I have wonderful news for thee. This little maid whom thou didst bring captive from the land of Israel hath told me strange news. In her country there lives a mighty man, a prophet called Elisha, who hath power to cure leprosy.

*Naaman.* What is this? Power to cure leprosy? Impossible!

*Mistress.* Oh, but it is true. She says that he has cured others, has even raised the dead. If he has cured others, can he not cure you? Oh, my lord, I beseech thee, make haste and go to him!

*Naaman.* This is a strange report. Speak, maid, how knowest thou this thing?

*Maiden.* Everyone in my country knows the prophet, for many are the people whom he hath helped. He is good to all and everyone doth love him. I pray, my lord, that thou wilt go to him for surely he can cure thee and bring again the smile to the face of my mistress. It grieves me to see her sorrowful.

*Naaman.* Thou art a good maid. If all that thou sayest is true and I am cured of this disease thou shalt not be forgotten, but shalt receive thy reward. [*Turning to wife.*] I go at once to make preparation for the journey. May it be even as we dare to hope!

[*Exit Naaman.*]

*Mistress.* Come with me. There is much to be done, Naaman must go at once.

[*Exeunt mistress and maid.*]

**CURTAIN**

## SCENE II

PLACE: *In front of Elisha's home. A sound as of horses stamping and noise of chariot and voices of men in distance. Near the door of the house stands Naaman, gorgeously dressed, and with him three attendants bearing gifts.*

*Naaman.* [*To first attendant.*] Hast thou a copy of the letter which the king did send to the king of Israel?

*Servant.* I have, my master.

*Naaman.* Strange; I thought this prophet would come out to meet me. Is he so used to visits from Captains of king's hosts that he cares not for our coming? [*To second attendant.*] What bearest thou?

*Attendant.* I have here, my lord, the ten talents of silver, and the six thousand pieces of gold which thou didst bring as a gift to the prophet.

*Naaman.* That is well. [*Addressing third attendant.*] What hast thou?

*Attendant.* I have here, my lord, the ten

changes of raiment which thou didst also bring as a present to the prophet.

*Naaman.* Knock. [*Attendant knocks; Gehazi opens the door.*] Where is thy master?

*Gehazi.* He is within. What is thy errand?

*Naaman.* Tell thy master that *Naaman,* captain of the host of the King of Syria, desires to see him. I have traveled from my own country that he might heal me of my leprosy. Bid him come forth. [*Exit Gehazi.*] I wonder what this prophet is like. Why doth he delay his coming? Perhaps he is not prepared to meet so mighty a person as the captain of the king's host.

[*Enter Gehazi.*

*Gehazi.* My master sayeth, Go and wash in the Jordan seven times and thy flesh shall come again to thee and thou shalt be clean.

*Naaman.* [*Angrily.*] What is the meaning of this? I thought, he will surely come out to see me and stand, and call on the name of the Lord his God, and strike his hand over the place and recover the leper. And now he maketh this strange condition. Are not the rivers of Damascus better than all the waters of Israel? May I not wash in them and be clean? I'll not go to the muddy waters of the Jordan.

*Attendants.* [*Timidly.*] My lord, hear me. If the prophet had bid thee do some great thing, wouldst thou not have done it? How much rather then, when he saith to thee, "Wash and be clean"?

*Naaman.* There is truth in what thou sayst. Come, let us go to the Jordan. I may as well do as the prophet says and see if anything comes of it, for I would be healed of this dread disease.

*[Exeunt.*

CURTAIN

## SCENE III

PLACE: *Same as Scene II. Enter Naaman and attendants bearing gifts. All are joyful and talking as they look upon Naaman.*

*Naaman.* Knock, for I would give my thanks to the prophet who hath healed me. Do not disturb him, leave the message and the gifts with his servant. Knock! [*Door opens; Elisha appears; Naaman bows low before him.*] O Elisha, thou servant of the living God. Behold, now I know that there is no God in all the earth, but in Israel; now, therefore, I pray thee, take a blessing of thy servant.

[*Attendant with gifts moves toward Elisha.*

*Elisha.* As the Lord liveth, before whom I stand, I will receive none.

*Naaman.* I pray thee, do not refuse. How can I depart into mine own land and not leave thee a token of my gratitude? Thou hast restored to me my life and thou hast shown me that Jehovah regardeth not the amount of a man's wealth but the value of his life. Anything I have is thine!

*Elisha.* I have my reward. Go thy way; as Jehovah hath blessed thee by increasing thy days, so must thou bless others by using well this life which has been restored.

*Naaman.* That will I do.

[*Exeunt Naaman and attendants.*

*Elisha.* Will the Lord be pleased with talents of silver and pieces of gold and changes of raiment? Ah, no, he asketh that man shall do justly, love mercy and walk humbly with his God. [*Looking in direction taken by Naaman.*] And that Naaman will do.

**CURTAIN**

# A WOMAN WHO DARED

CHARACTERS:
  Mordecai.
  Haman.
  Esther.
  King.
  Servants.
  Others.

## SCENE I

*Mordecai, servants and others in courtyard. Enter Haman.*

*Haman.* [*Soliloquizing.*] Ah, it is great to be the king's favorite! He hath promoted me above every other man. Now, when I appear, every knee doth bow to me, and every man doeth reverence to me even as to the king. [*Walks across the court. All except Mordecai bow low before him.*] Who is the man that doeth me no honor?

*Servant.* He is Mordecai, the Jew.

*Haman.* Why doth he refuse to kneel? Doth he not know that I am the king's favorite?

*Servant.* The Jews kneel before no one but their God.

*Haman.* He shall be punished.

*Servant.* Once he saved the king's life. One

day when he was sitting in the king's gate he overheard two of the king's chamberlains plotting against the king. He sent word to the king and when investigation was made it was discovered that the plans were all arranged and but for Mordecai's warning the king would have been slain that night.

*Haman.* What is that to me? Doubtless it is but a mere tale. No man shall refuse to honor me. He shall be punished. Ah, I have a plan.

[*Exit.*

CURTAIN

## SCENE II

PLACE: *King's palace, King seated on throne. Esther appears just within the entrance, unseen by King.*

*Esther.* Everyone knoweth that whosoever shall come unto the king, into the inner court, who is not called, shall be put to death, except such to whom the king shall hold out the golden sceptre, and I have not been called to come to the king for thirty days. Mordecai hath commanded me to do this thing. It is the only way to save my people. Mordecai and all my friends are praying for me. If I perish, I perish,—but I must see the king. Jehovah, help me!

[*Advances. King sees her, acts surprised, smiles, holds out sceptre.*

*King.* Esther, Esther, art thou come unto me?

[*Esther goes slowly near, touches top of sceptre.*]
Speak! What wilt thou, queen Esther? What is thy request? It shall be given thee to the half of the kingdom.

*Esther.* If it seem good unto the king, let the king and Haman come this day unto the banquet that I have prepared.

*King.* Thy request shall be granted. Haman and I will surely come.

**CURTAIN**

## SCENE III

PLACE: *A room in the Queen's house. Enter Esther, the king and Haman.*

*Esther.* Tarry yet a little while, O king, for now that the banquet is over, I would talk with thee.

*King.* Gladly will we tarry, for thou art fair and gracious, O queen. Tell me thy request, and it shall be granted thee even to half of the kingdom. [*King and Esther seat themselves.*

*Haman.* [*Half aloud.*] Esther did let no man come in with the king unto the banquet but myself. Yet all this availeth me nothing, so long as I see Mordecai, the Jew, sitting at the king's gate.

[*Seats himself.*

*King.* A strange thing happened last night. I could not sleep so I commanded that the book of records be read to me. There I found that one Mordecai had saved the king's life, but that no reward had been given him for the deed. Haman was without in the court. I had him called and I asked, "What shall be done unto the man whom the king delighteth to honor?" And Haman answered, "Let the royal robe be brought which the king useth to wear, and the horse that the king rideth upon, and the royal crown which is set upon his head. Let the man be arrayed and bring him on horseback through the streets of the city; let one of the noble princes go before him proclaiming, 'Thus shall it be done to the man whom the king delighteth to honor.'" All this was done unto Mordecai.

*Haman.* [*Aside.*] Yes, I said that, but I little thought he meant Mordecai. I thought it was myself of whom the king spoke.

*King.* Thou hast not yet told me thy request, Queen Esther.

*Esther.* Thou art kind, O king, and thy goodness to Mordecai doth make me bold. If I have found favor in thy sight, O King, grant that my life may be spared and my people also. For we are sold, I and my people to be destroyed, to be slain and to perish. Mordecai and I shall both perish for he of whom thou didst speak is my uncle. One who wishes harm to Mordecai hath betrayed us.

*King.* [*Angrily.*] What meanest thou? Who hath done this thing?

*Esther.* The enemy thou seest before thee. He is Haman.

[*Haman, frightened, falls on knees before queen.*

*Haman.* Oh, Queen Esther, spare me!

*King.* [*Clapping hands, calls to servant.*] Come at once. Take him away. Bring Mordecai to me! [*Exeunt servants and Haman.*] Thou art good as well as beautiful, O Queen. For thou didst think of thy people and not only of thyself. Thou and Mordecai shall be rewarded. [*Enter servants with Mordecai.*] Esther hath told me of the plot against thee and her people. Haman is punished. Thou shalt rule in his place. Take thou this ring which once I gave him. [*Passes to Mordecai.*] Thou shalt be next to me in the kingdom.

*Esther.* If it please the king, let an order go forth to reverse the letters sent out by Haman in which he wrote that all Jews in the King's provinces should be destroyed.

*King.* Mordecai shall write whatsoever thou commandest, and shall seal it with the king's ring. Not one of thy people shall perish. Mordecai did save the king's life, thou didst save thy people, shall the king do less? No harm shall befall them whom thou lovest. Mordecai shall see that the king's decree goeth forth.

*Esther.* Great is the king and good unto his Queen.

*Mordecai.* Great is the king and good unto all who serve him faithfully. [*Exit king.*] But greater is Jehovah who careth for his children and showeth them a way of escape from the enemy.

*Esther.* Blessed be his name for he heard and answered our prayers.

*Both.* Blessed be his holy name forever and ever.

**CURTAIN**

# THE OUTCOME OF A SECRET

CHARACTERS: Men, women, children, Bartimeus, Friend (*boy of same age as Bartimeus*).

## SCENE I

PLACE: *A village street, men, women and children passing to and fro. Blind Bartimeus sits by roadside begging. People drop coins into his cup.*

[*Enter friend.*

*Friend.* Ah, Bartimeus, how art thou to-day?
*Bartimeus.* Oh, I am so happy! I have a wonderful secret.
*Friend.* Happy? You, Bartimeus? What is this secret? Tell me the good news.
*Bartimeus.* I have been thinking of the great Teacher of whom everyone is talking. They say he doeth marvelous things. Not only doth he teach and tell beautiful stories, but I have been told that he heals the sick.
*Friend.* Yes, I have heard so, too.
*Bartimeus.* I know he does because I heard one of his followers tell how he healed a deaf and dumb boy. The boy could not speak plainly. It was hard for anyone but his mother to understand him. They brought the boy to the great Teacher. He took him aside from the crowd, he

talked with him, he put his fingers into his ears, he prayed to God, and when they returned the boy could talk. The man said the boy was so happy he talked all the time.

*Friend.* It certainly is strange. He is unlike any other man.

*Bartimeus.* But I have not told you the secret yet. If he can make a deaf and dumb boy hear and speak, why can't he make a blind person see?

*Friend.* Oh—but you have always been blind. Then, too, he has never seen you.

*Bartimeus.* I know, but though I have always wanted to see, I never tried before to help myself to obtain sight. Now I am going to do my part.

*Friend.* But you can't go to the Teacher. You don't know where he is.

*Bartimeus.* No, but here is my secret. The man told me that he thought the Teacher would pass this way soon, as he is on his way to Jericho. So every day I sit and listen for his coming. I shall know by the excitement. I shall hear the people exclaim and hurry by to see him. Oh, if he would only come soon!

*Friend.* Maybe he is coming now. I see a company of people coming over the hill.

*Bartimeus.* [*Rising from seat.*] Oh, Oh! Is it he? Is it? Is he really coming? Oh, let us go out to meet them. I must not miss him. [*Boys hastily leave stage; Bartimeus cries out.*] Thou Son of David, have mercy on me! Have mercy on me, Thou Son of David. Make me to see!

CURTAIN

## SCENE II

PLACE: *Same as Scene I.*

[*Enter friend.*

*Friend.* It seems strange not to see Blind Bartimeus sitting here begging. I wonder where he is. He said he would meet me here to-day and tell me all about what happened. To think that he can really see!

[*Enter Bartimeus walking rapidly.*

*Bartimeus.* Ah, Friend, you are here first. There was so much to see by the way that I stopped often. How wonderful it is to be able to see! In all the years that we have been friends, I never saw your face until yesterday. I can hardly believe it is true! I never saw the grass, the sky, the water before.

*Friend.* Tell me what happened. You ran so fast and went into the crowd where I could not follow you.

*Bartimeus.* I know, but I had to see him. I did not dare wait until he saw me. As I ran I cried to him, "Have mercy upon me, thou Son of David." The people tried to make me keep still. Some said, "Don't bother the great Teacher." Others said, "He won't stop for you. He is going to speak to the multitude." Many said, "Keep still, and go away." But I only cried the louder. Suddenly the people all seemed to stand still and all stopped talking. It was very quiet. I called again. Then a voice, close to me said, "Be of good cheer, he calleth thee." And a man took me by the hand and led me still farther into the crowd. At last I stood in front of the Teacher. He said, "What wilt thou that I should do unto thee?" It was the sweetest voice I ever heard. I answered, "Lord, that I might receive my sight." Then he said, "Go thy way, thy faith hath made thee whole." And suddenly my eyes were open. The first sight I beheld was his face. Oh, the beauty, the kindness, and the love in it! The Teacher began to move on and I followed him. The crowd grew in numbers but I kept close to him and sometimes he talked to me.

*Friend.* What did he say?

*Bartimeus.* He said he was glad to help me because I had tried hard to help myself. He said that as he had helped me, I must help others. I asked him if I could not stay with him, but he said I must return home and be his disciple here in Jericho. He needed followers in every place and I could help him most by remaining here in a city where he could not stay. So, though I am here and he is far away, I shall always be his follower.

*Friend.* And I, too.

*Bartimeus.* We will go together, telling others of the great Teacher, for I would have every one know him as I do.

*Friend.* Let us go to the group down the street and tell them the wonderful news.

[*Boys leave stage.*

*Bartimeus.* [*Saying as he goes.*] Once I was blind. Now I see. I'm glad I did my part.

CURTAIN

# EASTER MORN

BY ANNIE M. DARLING
(A member of my Story Telling Class)

CHARACTERS:
Pilate, chief priests, and Pharisees.
Mary Magdalene.
Salome.
Mary, Mother of James.
Peter.
John.
Group of people.

## SCENE I

PLACE: *Pilate's house.*

*Chief priest.* Sir, thou hast done well to put to death that impostor, Jesus, who called himself the King of the Jews, and hast showed thyself a true friend to Cæsar. Jesus is indeed dead, but strange things have happened since his death—earthquakes, and darkness at mid-day, the veil of our temple has been rent in twain. These things have brought to mind the saying of that deceiver that three days after his death he will rise again. The people are already beginning to talk and whisper among themselves that perhaps this man was a prophet. His disciples are still in the city and will do all things possible to keep alive in the hearts of the people the belief that this man is the Messiah. We have therefore a request to make. Joseph of Arimathæa has taken the body and placed it in his own new tomb, wherein no man was ever yet laid. Command thou that the sepulchre be made sure or his disciples will come in the night and steal away the body, telling the people that he has risen from the dead. The last error will thus be worse than the first.

*Pilate.* [*Superciliously.*] Thou hast a watch. Go thy way. Make the sepulchre as sure as ye can. Seal the stone with the Roman seal and set a guard around it. The grave of thy king should indeed be guarded.

[*The chief priests go out.*

*Pilate.* [*Sadly.*] How they hate him even in death. He was a good man and a just man. How sadly and forgivingly he looked at me when I delivered him to the Jews. [*Looking at his hands.*] I washed my hands of all blood-guiltiness but methinks they seem dyed with innocent blood. What if he were in truth a prophet and a king! Will he indeed rise again,—even from the dead? It troubleth me. [*Goes out with head bowed.*

## SCENE II

PLACE: *Room in an Oriental house. Dim light, curtains drawn. A single lamp burning, for it is just before dawn.*

[*Enter Mary Magdalene.*

*Mary.* Those dear hands and feet are pierced and bleeding, though they did no wrong except to bring love and healing to sick and sorrowful ones. Never again shall I hear His voice say, "Mary, thy sins are forgiven thee," or feel His hand placed on my head in blessing. My heart is full of sorrow, but all I can do for Him is to bring these few spices to His resting place.

[*Enter Salome.*

*Salome.* Art thou ready? Mary, the mother of James, is on the way and will soon join us. Thou hast the spices and I have the ointments here. And yet there is so little that we can do for Him who did so much for us. Oh, that we might see Him among us once more, with His dear smile, His ready words of sympathy for all of our perplexities. How the poor, the sick, the sinful thronged about Him, and all went away comforted. Our Messiah! I cannot think Him dead! And yet we go to anoint His body!

[*Enter Mary, the mother of James.*

*Mary, the mother of James.* Are we all gathered? But I have sad news for you. All our plans may be vain, for I have just heard that the chief priests and the Pharisees have been to Pilate, and asked him to set a guard about the tomb. They have sealed it with the Roman seal and put a guard of soldiers about it. How can we roll away that great stone and persuade those rough soldiers to let us anoint the dear body of our Lord? May we not do even this to show our love for Him who gave His life for us?

*Salome.* Thy story may be but a rumor. There must be some way, for love overcometh all difficulties. Let us go at once; the dawn cometh and it will soon be bright day.

[*The women go out.*

CURTAIN

## SCENE III

PLACE: *Same Oriental room. There is only a flicker of light from the lamp; the daylight streams in through the curtains.*

[*The door opens and Peter and John come in. Peter's head is bowed in sorrow, and John's arm is placed lovingly about his shoulders.*

*Peter.* And I denied Him! I, who said though all others should leave Him, I would be with Him. Those loving eyes I see ever before me,—so sad, so sorrowful. Why did my tongue speak so hastily? I was not afraid to walk on the water when He bade me, but I could not face a little serving maid and own that He was my loving Master. And I denied Him, not once, or twice, but thrice, even as He said. My sin is beyond forgiveness.

*John.* Oh, say not so, Peter. Did not the Master say to forgive seventy times seven? And hath He not said He loved thee? He knoweth thee, Peter, that thou hast a hasty and impetuous tongue, but a warm and loving heart.

How can we live without Him after these three years of daily sympathetic companionship! How He hath cheered us as we walked over the long and weary roads of Galilee; how His words have made our hearts burn within us. Have we lost forever our loving Master, our Messiah? I cannot believe Him dead. He said once: "In three days I shall rise again." What did He mean? Is it possible He will come back to us, He whom we saw hanging on the cross, whose body we saw Joseph lay away in the tomb?

*Peter.* The women have gone this morning to prepare Him with sweet spices and ointments for His burial. But I am not worthy to go near even His dead body.

[*The sound of women's voices comes through the open window. Enter Salome, and Mary, the mother of James.*

*Salome.* [*Speaks hurriedly, almost breathlessly.*] He is gone. He is not there. We went to the tomb, with our spices and ointments, wondering how we could roll away the stone, for we had heard that a seal had been set and a guard placed around the tomb. And lo, when we reached it, the stone was rolled away. The tomb was empty. We went in, and saw not our dear Lord but an angel clothed in white garments. We were afraid and knew not what to say. And the angel said: "Ye seek Jesus of Nazareth who was crucified. He is not here. He is risen. Behold the place where they laid Him. But go your way and tell His disciples, and Peter [*turning to Peter*], he said to tell you especially, Peter, that He goeth before you into Galilee. There shall ye see Him even as He said.

*Peter.* [*To John.*] Let us go to the tomb. I cannot believe unless I see.

[*Peter and John go out quickly.*

*Salome.* We went forth in sorrow and are returned rejoicing. We went weeping and lo, we come again bearing tidings of great joy.

[*Enter Mary Magdalene, hastily.*

*Mary Magdalene.* I have seen the Lord!

*Salome and Mary, the mother of James.* [*Together.*] Seen the Lord—where?

*Mary Magdalene.* In the garden near the tomb. I lingered behind, for I could not bear to leave the place where my dear Lord had lain. I could not believe it was really true that He had risen. I feared they had stolen Him away. Then I heard a voice, but when I looked up and saw a man standing there, I thought it was the gardener, for my eyes were blinded with tears. Then He said, "*Mary,*" and I knew Him for my dear Master. I fell at His feet, crying "Rabboni," and He said: "Touch me not, for I am not yet ascended unto my Father; but go and tell my disciples and say unto them, I ascend unto my Father and your Father, and to my God and your God."

[*Enter Peter and John.*

*Peter.* It is even as thou hast said. We ran to the tomb and found it empty. I went in, but there were only the linen clothes lying folded at one side; my Master was not there. He hath risen even as He said. He is not dead. He liveth! Alleluia!

*Salome.* [*In awed tones, rising to exultation.*]

## EASTER MORN

Christ is risen indeed. We shall see Him yet again, for Mary hath seen Him and He hath told her to tell His disciples that He liveth. He who was dead is alive, alive for evermore. Death could not hold him. It hath no more dominion over Him. He hath loosed the bands of mortality and put on immortality. Through the grave, the gate of death, He hath passed to joyful resurrection. He is risen from the dead and become the first fruits of them that sleep. He hath overcome death; He hath opened unto us the gate of everlasting life; by man came death, by man cometh also the resurrection from the dead; in Christ shall all be made alive. Alleluia! Alleluia! Blessed be the name of the Lord.

> [*While the women and disciples have been speaking, men, women, young men and maidens, and even boys and girls have entered one after another, until a company has gathered. As Salome ceases speaking, a young girl or young boy steps to the front and bursts forth into the triumphant Easter Song, "Christ the Lord is risen to-day." The whole company join in the Alleluias, and after the first verse all sing. They file slowly down the length of the church (centre) singing, with heads lifted, and pass out, the song gradually dying away in the distance. The soloist should preferably be a boy tenor, and the singing of the company should be a glorious swelling chorus of rev-*

*erent joy. Possibly the people who enter later might come bearing Easter lilies. If the company should include some of all ages from young boys and girls to old age, it would bring home more clearly, possibly, to those who had loved and lost dear ones, that the hope of Resurrection is for all, for death touches all periods of life.]*

**CURTAIN**

## EASTER MORNING

[*An arrangement of the previous story given in one scene for use in a room where screens or curtain are not available. This was presented at service given in a church auditorium on Easter Sunday. The decorations of palms and flowers gave the effect of a garden.*]

CHARACTERS:
 Mary Magdalene.
 Salome.
 Mary, Mother of James.
 Peter.
 John.
 Young Woman Soloist.
 Group of People: men, women, boys, girls.
 Leader of Group.

SCENE: *A Garden.*

*Mary.* My heart is full of sorrow. They have crucified our Lord and now He lieth in the tomb, and we can do nothing for Him but take the spices and ointment for His body. Those dear hands and feet, pierced and bleeding, which did no wrong but rather brought love and healing to sick and sorrowful ones. Never again shall I hear His voice say, "Mary, thy sins are forgiven thee," or feel His hand placed on my head in blessing. All I can do is to take these few spices to His resting place.

[*Enter Salome.*

*Salome.* Art thou ready, Mary Magdalene? Mary, the mother of James, is on the way and will join us. Hast thou the spices? I have the ointment here. It is so little we can do for Him who did so much for us. Oh, that we might see Him among us once more. His dear smile, His ready words of sympathy for all our perplexities. How the poor, the sick, the sinful thronged around Him, and all went away comforted. Our Lord, our Messiah! I cannot think Him dead, and yet we go to anoint His body.

[*Enter Mary, the Mother of James.*

*Mary.* Are we all gathered? But I have sad news for you. All our plans may be in vain, for I have just heard that the chief priests and the Pharisees have been to Pilate and asked him to set a guard about the tomb. They have sealed it with the Roman seal and put a guard of soldiers about it. How can we roll away that great stone and persuade those rough soldiers to let us anoint the dear body of our Lord? May we not do even this to show our love for Him who gave His life for us?

*Salome.* The story may be but a rumor. There must be some way, for love overcometh all difficulties. Let us go at once; the dawn cometh and it will soon be bright day. [*The women go out.*

## EASTER MORNING

[*Enter Peter and John. Peter's head is bowed in sorrow and John's arm is placed lovingly about his shoulders.*

*Peter.* And I denied Him! I, who said though all others should leave Him I would be with Him. Those loving eyes I see ever before me,—so sad, so sorrowful! Why did my tongue speak so hastily? I was not afraid to walk on the water when He bade me, but I could not face a little serving maid and own that He was my loving Master. And I denied Him! Not once or twice, but thrice, even as He said. My sin is beyond forgiveness!

*John.* Oh, say not so, Peter. Didst not the Master say to forgive seventy times seven? And hath He not said He loved thee? He knoweth thee, Peter, that thou hast a hasty and impetuous tongue, but a warm and loving heart.

How can we live without Him after these three years of daily sympathetic companionship? How He hath cheered us as we walked over the long and weary roads of Galilee; how His words have made our hearts burn within us! Have we lost forever our loving Master, our Messiah! I cannot believe Him dead. He said once: "In three days, I shall rise again." What did He mean? Is it possible He will come back to us? Jesus, whom we saw hanging on the cross, whose body we saw Joseph lay away in the tomb.

*Peter.* The women have gone this morning to prepare Him with sweet spices and ointment for His burial. But I am not worthy to go near even His dead body!

[*The sound of women's voices is heard. Enter Salome, and Mary, the mother of James.*

*Salome.* [*Speaks hurriedly and almost breathlessly.*] He is gone! He is not there! We went to the tomb with our spices and ointments wondering how we should roll away the stone, for we heard that a seal had been set and a guard placed around the tomb. And lo! when we reached it, the stone was rolled away. The tomb was empty, we went in, and we saw not our Lord, but an angel clothed in white garments. We were afraid and knew not what to say, and the angel said, "Ye seek Jesus of Nazareth who was crucified. He is not here. He is risen. Behold the place where they laid Him. But go your way and tell His disciples, and Peter [*turning to Peter*], he said to tell you especially, Peter, that "He goeth before you into Galilee. There shall ye see Him even as He said."

*Peter.* [*To John.*] Let us go to the tomb. I cannot believe unless I see.

[*Peter and John hastily withdraw.*

*Mary.* We went forth in sorrow and are returned rejoicing. We went weeping and lo! we come again bearing tidings of great joy.

[*Enter Mary Magdalene hastily.*

*Mary Magdalene.* I have seen the Lord!

*Salome and other Mary.* [*Together.*] Seen the Lord! Where?

*Mary Magdalene.* In the garden near the tomb. I lingered behind, for I could not bear to leave the place where my dear Lord had lain. I could not believe it was really true that He had risen.

I feared that they had stolen Him away. Then I heard a voice, and when I looked up I saw a man standing there. I thought it was the gardener, for my eyes were blinded with tears. Then He said, "Mary," and I knew Him for my dear Master. I fell at His feet crying, "Rabboni," and He said, "Touch me not, for I am not yet ascended unto my Father, but go and tell my disciples and say unto them, 'I ascend unto my Father and your Father and to my God and your God.'"

[*Enter Peter and John.*

*Peter.* It is even as thou hast said. We ran to the tomb and found it empty. I went in, but there were only the linen clothes lying folded at one side; my Master was not there. He hath risen even as He said! He is not dead! He liveth! Alleluia!

*Mary.\** [*Lights turned on the cross.*] The cross! All these hours I have thought of it with horror, as I saw again our Lord hanging there! But now all is changed and I see the cross illumined with the glory of the love that gave to us God's best; and through all the ages to come the cross shall be the symbol of all followers of our Lord and Christ.

*Salome.* [*In awed tones rising to exultation.*] Christ is risen! He liveth indeed! Mary hath seen Him! He hath talked with her and hath told her

---

\* May be omitted if preferred. Many churches have an illuminated cross which could be used at this point.

to tell His disciples. We shall see Him yet again. He who was dead is alive for evermore! Death could not hold Him! He hath loosed the bands of mortality and has put on immortality. Through the grave, the gate of death, He hath passed to joyful resurrection! He is risen from the dead and become the first fruits of them that slept. He hath overcome death! He hath opened unto us the gate of everlasting life. By man came death, by man came also the resurrection from the dead; in Christ shall all be made alive. No longer shall men sorrow without hope. He is the resurrection and the life! Alleluia! Blessed be the name of the Lord!

[*Enter group of boys and girls, men and women bringing flowers, if possible.*

*Leader.* Then there is hope for all mankind, old or young, whom we represent, who through all the ages must see their friends pass on into what we call death, and must themselves finally yield up this mortal life.

*Mary.* In Christ shall all be made alive.

*Girl.* [*Sings.*]

"Jesus Christ is Risen To-day, Alleluia!"

[*Group on platform join in the Alleluias of first stanza. In second stanza Junior and Choral choirs, stationed in rear of room, give the Alleluia. On next, choirs, soloists, and group on platform all sing. While persons are leaving platform choirs alone repeat first stanzas. At the close every one will have disappeared from platform.*

# A SEARCH FOR A WIFE

CHARACTERS:
Abraham.
Isaac.
Eliezer, *Abraham's servant.*
Rebekah, *a maiden of Mesopotamia.*
Bethuel, *Rebekah's father.*
Laban, *Rebekah's brother.*

## SCENE I

PLACE: *Abraham's tent. Abraham sitting in front of tent.*

*Abraham.* The years of my life have been many, but through them all the Lord hath blessed me. Now I know that my days can not be long in this land and soon I shall leave my kindred and friends. Before that time I would find a wife for Isaac, my son. All about are the women of the Canaanites, but my son's wife must be of his own people and yet there are no Israelitish maidens near. Eliezer must help me. Ho, Eliezer!

[*Enter Eliezer.*

*Eliezer.* Didst thou call?

*Abraham.* Long thou hast been my servant and thou hast proven trustworthy. Now I would entrust to thy care a matter of great importance.

Isaac must have a wife. I am too old to seek for her. Thou must do it for me.

*Eliezer.* Where shall I seek her, among the women of Canaan?

*Abraham.* Not there. Promise me by the Lord, the God of heaven and earth that thou wilt not take a wife for my son of the daughters of the Canaanites among whom we dwell?

*Eliezer.* Where then shall I seek her?

*Abraham.* I would have thee go unto my country and to my kindred, and there find an Israelitish maiden.

*Eliezer.* Peradventure, the woman will not be willing to follow me unto this land. What shall I do then?

*Abraham.* The Lord God of heaven which took me from my father's house, and from the land of my kindred, and which spake unto me and that sware unto me, saying, Unto thy children will I give this land, he shall send his angel before thee; and thou shalt take a wife for my son from thence. If the woman be not willing to follow thee, thou shalt be free from thy promise. [*Enters tent.*

*Eliezer.* This is a serious matter, but I have promised. The Lord help me in my task. I will prepare the camels for the journey, the gifts for the maiden and make provision for her return. It is a long way to Mesopotamia. [*Exit.*

**CURTAIN**

## SCENE II

PLACE: *A well in a country. Ferns and palms, etc., may be used.*

*Eliezer.* At last I am in Mesopotamia. It was a long journey. Many times my courage well nigh failed me. Now that I am here I know not how to find the maid. O Lord God of my master Abraham, I pray Thee send me help this day. Behold I stand here by the well, and the daughters of the city come to draw water. Let it come to pass that the damsel to whom I shall say, "Let down thy pitcher, I pray thee, that I may drink"; and she shall say, "Drink and I will give thy camels drink also"; let the same be she that thou hast appointed for thy servant.

[*Eliezer stands near well. Enter Rebekah, carrying pitcher. Goes to well.*

*Eliezer.* Let me, I pray thee, drink a little water out of the pitcher.

*Rebekah.* Drink, my lord. [*Eliezer takes pitcher and drinks.*] I will draw water for thy camels, also, until they have done drinking.

[*Goes to well.*

*Eliezer.* Tell me first, whose daughter art thou?

*Rebekah.* I am the daughter of Bethuel.

*Eliezer.* Thou art both kind and fair. Take these gifts. [*Offers her presents.*] Is there room in thy father's house for us to lodge?

*Rebekah.* We have both straw and provender enough, and room to lodge in.

*Eliezer.* Go tell thy father that my master Abraham hath sent me hither and I would see him.

*Rebekah.* I will tell my father. [*Exit.*

*Eliezer.* Blessed be the Lord God of my master Abraham, who hath led me to this place.

[*Enter Rebekah, Bethuel and Laban.*

*Laban.* Why waitest thou here? The damsel hath told us of thee. I have prepared thy house and room for thy camels.

*Eliezer.* I will not eat until I have told my errand. I am Abraham's servant. The Lord hath blessed my master greatly and hath given him great possessions of flocks, herds, silver and gold. He hath one greatly beloved son, Isaac, unto whom he hath given all that he hath. My master made me promise that I would go unto the land of his kindred and there find a wife for Isaac, lest he be tempted to marry one of the women of Canaan. I came this day unto the well, and as I stood there I prayed, O Lord, let it come to pass that when a virgin cometh forth to draw water, and I say unto her, Give me, I pray thee, a little water of thy pitcher, to drink, and she say to me, Drink thou and I will draw water for thy camels also; let the same be the one thou hast appointed for my master's son. Before I had done speaking Rebekah came unto the well and said even the words I had asked of the Lord, and when she told me that she was the daughter of Bethuel, I knew that I had come to the right place. Tell me now, if ye will deal kindly with my master, and if not tell me, that I may seek farther.

*Bethuel.* The thing cometh from the Lord.
*Laban.* We cannot speak unto thee bad or good.
*Bethuel.* Behold, Rebekah is before thee, take her, and go, and let her be thy master's son's wife, even the wife of Isaac.
*Eliezer.* God hath answered my prayer and that of my master. Take, I pray thee, these gifts.
[*Gives gifts unto Rebekah and Bethuel and Laban.*

CURTAIN

## SCENE III

PLACE: *Same as Scene I. Abraham in front of tent.*

*Abraham.* Yonder, I saw camels approaching. Can it be that Eliezer returneth so soon? I wonder whom he is bringing with him.
[*Enter Eliezer, Rebekah and Isaac.*
*Eliezer.* Oh, Master, I have done even as thou hath said. Behold the damsel, Rebekah, the daughter of Bethuel.
*Isaac.* As I was meditating in the fields just now, it being eventide, I lifted up my eyes and beheld the camels approaching. When this woman lighted off her camel, I knew that Eliezer had prospered in his search. I joined myself to the company and learned of the journey, the damsel and her willingness to come hither. Now, O my father, we await thy approval.
*Abraham.* [*To damsel.*] Thou art good to

leave thy home and thy kindred, and journey to a far country. Isaac shall make thee happy and the Lord shall bless you both. [*Turns to Isaac.*] Show her to her tent. She must be weary after her long journey. [*Exeunt Rebekah and Isaac. Abraham to Eliezer.*] Thou hast done well. Come with me for I would hear how the Lord prospered thee on thy journey.

[*Exeunt Abraham and Eliezer.*]

**CURTAIN**

# THE VALUE OF PREPARATION

CHARACTERS:
Ten young women.
A herald.
A group of people.

### SCENE I

[*Enter five maidens.*]

*First Virgin.* Where are the others?
*Second Virgin.* They stopped for oil.
*Third Virgin.* Why do they wish to carry any more? Surely we have enough. It is almost time for the bridegroom.
*Fourth Virgin.* [*Seating herself.*] Shall we wait here?

[*All sit. Enter five other maidens.*]

*Fifth Virgin.* Well, here you are. We feared you would be late.
*Sixth Virgin.* We purchased more oil and filled our lamps.
*Third Virgin.* Surely we have enough. Why buy more?
*Seventh Virgin.* We did not want our lights to go out before our return.
*Fourth Virgin.* You are always over-anxious. You plan for what may never happen. Why not

enjoy the present instead of thinking about the future?

*Seventh Virgin.* We would be ready for what the future may bring. We would be prepared for any event.

*First Virgin.* The bridegroom delayeth his coming. Let us rest awhile.

[*All assume positions of rest. Quiet reigns, soft lullaby played on violin from behind scene. As music ceases, a herald enters.*

*Herald.* Awake, awake! The bridegroom cometh. Go ye out to meet him.

[*Virgins arise hastily. Lights of first five are out.*

*Five Virgins.* Our lamps are gone out!

*First Virgin.* Give us some of your oil!

*Second Virgin.* Yes, you bought extra. Give us of your supply.

*Eighth Virgin.* Not so, lest there be not enough for us and for you.

*Second Virgin.* Oh, give us some!

*Third Virgin.* Yes, yes, if only a little!

*Ninth Virgin.* We have none to spare. If we give to you all the lamps will go out.

*Tenth Vrgin.* Go ye to them that sell, and buy for yourselves.

*Fifth Virgin.* The way is far and the bridegroom cometh.

*Third Virgin.* Well, if we are to have oil, we must go for it. Come, let us hasten lest the bridegroom come and we be not here.

[*Exeunt five virgins.*

## THE VALUE OF PREPARATION

*Tenth Virgin.* I am sorry for them.

*Ninth Virgin.* I would gladly have given of my oil if I could have spared any.

*Seventh Virgin.* I wonder if they would call me over-anxious now. It pays to be ready. For at a time when we think not opportunity cometh even as the bridegroom to-night.

*Eighth Virgin.* The bridegroom cometh nearer. Let us who are ready go into the marriage.

**CURTAIN**

### SCENE II

PLACE: *Large doorway in house. People entering. At rear of group come the five wise virgins.*

*Sixth Virgin.* Ah, we are just in time!

*Seventh Virgin.* Had we waited longer we should have been too late for as soon as the bridegroom enters the door is closed.

*Eighth Virgin.* [*Looking back.*] I cannot see the others.

*Ninth Virgin.* It pays to be ready.

*Tenth Virgin.* Yes, it pays to be ready.

[*Party enters; door is closed. Sound of music, talking and laughter comes from within.*

[*Enter five foolish virgins, hurrying.*

*First Virgin.* Oh, I hope we are in time.

*Second Virgin.* I am so tired. We hurried so.

[61]

*Third Virgin.* If only we had filled our lamps when the others did.

*Fourth Virgin.* Well, maybe it does pay to be ready.

*Fifth Virgin.* Look, the door is shut!

ALL. Oh, oh, oh! [*Hasten to door, knock on it.*] Open, open unto us!

*Voice.* [*From within.*] Who are you?

*First Virgin.* Friends, invited to the marriage.

*Voice.* That cannot be. The friends of the bridegroom are with him.

*Third Virgin.* Open the door and thou shalt see.

ALL. Yes, yes, open the door.

*Voice.* Depart, I know you not.

[*Virgins turn away with sorrowful looks. Just before leaving the platform all turn and look back.*]

*First Virgin.* They that were ready went in. Yes, it pays to be ready.

ALL. [*Softly.*] It pays to be ready.

CURTAIN

# THE SECRET OF SUCCESS

CHARACTERS:
 Nehemiah.
 Jews.
 King.
 Queen.
 Hanani.
 Musicians.
 Servants.
 Ezra.

## SCENE I

PLACE: *A room in the king's house. Nehemiah preparing wine for the king.*

*Nehemiah.* Strange that I, a Jew, should be the trusted servant of the Persian King. It is not often true that foreigners, conquered subjects, are trusted above the king's own servants. Yet so it is with me. Artaxerxes, the king, doth require me to prepare his wine and take it to him each day. No one else will he permit to prepare the juice, lest an enemy should put poison in the glass. The king is good to me, but would I were free, that I might return to my own land! If only I might see the temple which the returned Jews are building. Gladly would I do my part, I would work, I would suffer, yea, I would be willing to go hungry if I might but return to my native land.

[*Enter Hanani and two Jews.*

*Hanani.* Ah, brother, we greet you.

[*Nehemiah goes to meet them.*

*Nehemiah.* Glad, indeed, am I to see you. Tell me, how goes it with our brethren at Jerusalem?

[*Men look sad, shake heads.*

*Hanani.* Not very well.

*Nehemiah.* What do you mean?

*Hanani.* The wall of the city is broken down.

*First Jew.* The gates thereof are burned with fire.

*Second Jew.* The people are in great affliction and are becoming discouraged.

*Nehemiah.* Would I were with them, but here I am, a captive. Oh Jerusalem, Jerusalem, the home of my fathers, my native land!

[*Seats himself, buries head in hands.*

*Hanani.* Surely there must be help for our people. God can not have forsaken us.

*Nehemiah.* [*Looking up.*] Think you, that if we beseech him most earnestly, he will hear our cry?

*First Jew.* The people do not seem to know how.

*Second Jew.* They have no king.

*Nehemiah.* The Lord hath promised to remember his people and to bless all who keep his commandments.

*Hanani.* Ah, that may be the cause of our trouble. We have often forgotten his commandments. We have not always done the things we knew. We have grown discouraged and weak. We have waited for God to do the work for us;

we have not helped ourselves; we have not used the knowledge and power which he hath given us.

*Nehemiah.* Let us pray unto God, night and day, that he will forgive the Children of Israel for their neglect and that he will cause them to remember the things which Moses, Joshua and other great men have spoken. Return ye to Jerusalem. Bid the people to pray and to work. I will also pray that God will hear your prayers and fulfil his promise, when he said: If ye transgress I will scatter you abroad among the nations: But if ye return unto me, and keep my commandments, and do them, I will bring you from the uttermost places of the earth and set you in the place which I have chosen for you.

*Hanani.* Yes, let us be going.

*Nehemiah.* And the blessing of God go with you.

*Hanani.* And may the blessing of God remain with you.

[*Nehemiah in attitude of deep thought.*
[*Exeunt Hanani and friends.*

CURTAIN

## SCENE II

PLACE: *The king's room. King and queen seated near each other. Musicians playing for them. As music ceases, king speaks to servant.*

*King.* I would have my wine. Call Nehemiah.
[*Exit servant.*

*Queen.* Thou art very fond of thy cup-bearer.

*King.* Well I may be for he is faithful and trustworthy. Although a captive, he can be trusted beyond any of my own people. There is something in his face that makes me know he is true.

*Queen.* Thou art indeed fortunate to have even one of whom thou art sure. He comes.

[*Enter Nehemiah. Nehemiah on bended knee presents the wine to the king.*

*King.* [*Takes glass.*] Why is thy countenance sad? Art thou sick?

*Nehemiah.* Nay, my lord, thy servant is not sick.

*King.* Then nothing but sorrow of heart can cause thee to look so sad.

[*Nehemiah bows his head low but does not speak.*

*King.* Speak. Is aught troubling thee?

*Nehemiah.* Let the King live forever; why should not my countenance be sad, when the city, the place of my fathers' sepulchres, lieth waste and the gates thereof are consumed with fire.

*King.* For what dost thou make request? What can I do for thee?

*Nehemiah.* If it please the king and if thy servant hath found favor in thy sight, send me into Judah, unto the city of my fathers, that I may build it.

*King.* If I let thee go, wilt thou return unto me?

*Nehemiah.* When my work is finished or whenever the king shall need me, I will return.

*Queen.* Thou must let him go, else he will grieve and grow sick even in thy service.

*King.* I can ill spare thee and thy stay must be brief.

*Nehemiah.* Yes, oh king.

*King.* Thou shalt go. Is there any help I can give thee for thy journey or for thy work?

*Nehemiah.* If it please the king, let letters be given me to the governors beyond the Euphrates River, telling them to allow me to pass through their countries to Judah.

*King.* It shall be done.

*Queen.* Thou couldst give to him, O king, a letter to Asaph, the keeper of the king's forests in Judea, that he may give to Nehemiah the wood he needs for the gates of the city and for the house wherein he shall live.

*King.* It shall be, even as thou sayest, O queen.

*Nehemiah.* Thou art kind to thy cup-bearer.

*King.* Take with thee camels, laden with all the things thou dost require. There shall accompany thee, soldiers and horsemen, all that is necessary for the journey shall be provided.

*Nehemiah.* May God reward thee for granting thy servant's desire. May peace and prosperity be thine. [*Exit.*

*King.* I will go, myself, to see that the letters are prepared.

*Queen.* I will go, also. There may be something I can do for the king's favorite.

[*Exeunt king and queen.*

CURTAIN

## SCENE III

PLACE: *Night, outside wall of Jerusalem.*
*Nehemiah and four friends come from city. Nehemiah leaves friends. Walks along wall examining it here and there.*

*First Friend.* [*In low tone.*] How strangely Nehemiah acts.

*Second Friend.* What is he searching for?

*Third Friend.* Why look by night?

*Fourth Friend.* Yes, why did he bring us here at night?

*First Friend.* I tried to make him tell me his plan.

*Others.* So did I.

*First Friend.* He is returning, perhaps he will tell us.

[*Nehemiah joins group.*

*Second Friend.* Did you find what you were seeking?

*Third Friend.* Why all this mystery? Tell us what you are doing.

*Nehemiah.* Let us sit down and I will tell you. No one is near; we shall not be overheard.

[*All seat themselves.*

*Nehemiah.* Even while I was in Persia I heard of the conditions of Jerusalem, but I wanted to see for myself. Now, I know what you have already seen. The walls are broken down, the gates are burned, the towers are broken and the stones are in heaps where they were thrown by the soldiers.

## THE SECRET OF SUCCESS

One can enter the city at any time and through many different openings. There is no protection from robbers or enemies.

*Fourth Friend.* We all know that. Why bring us out here at night to tell us about it?

*Nehemiah.* Listen. I have a plan. We can rebuild the walls. Artaxerxes will help us. Already he has given me a letter to the keeper of his forest in Judea, telling him to allow us to have all the wood we need for the gates. My plan is to secure a promise from the nobles of the cities, from the rulers of the country, from the priests, from the merchants, from the goldsmiths, and from all the workmen, that each will be responsible for a certain part of the wall to rebuild it. Towns and cities will do the same. The rich shall build the portion of the wall near their own houses; every one shall help and we shall see the sheep gate, the water gate, the old gate, the valley gate, the towers, the fountain, the pool, and the king's house rebuilt and made strong once more. Ye see the distress that we are in,—how Jerusalem lieth waste, and the gates thereof are burned with fire; come, and let us build up the wall of Jerusalem, that we be no more a reproach.

*First Friend.* It is a good plan. I believe we can do it.

*Second Friend.* I think so. Let us go into the city and on the morrow tell the good news to all the people.

*Third Friend.* Let us rise up and build.

*Fourth Friend.* Yes, let us rise up and build.

*All.* [*Joyfully.*] Let us rise up and build.

*Nehemiah.* The God of Heaven will prosper us: therefore we his servants will arise and build. Come, let us return.

[*Exeunt all.*

CURTAIN

## SCENE IV

PLACE: *A street, elevated platform at one side. Many people walking and talking together. Hanani, Ezra, and Nehemiah near platform.*

*Hanani.* Thy work is accomplished. The walls are rebuilt and once more the people are protected from enemies.

*Nehemiah.* Yes, the walls are built and the gates made new, even the towers are as of old. Many were the discouragements but God hath blessed our efforts.

*Hanani.* How terrified we were when we heard that the Arabians and the Ammonites and all our enemies had conspired together to come and fight against Jerusalem.

*Ezra.* I can see the people now as they stood talking together, terrified at the news that the enemy was preparing to come against us; I see Nehemiah as he walked into the crowd. Instantly the talking ceased; every eye was upon him. Nehemiah spoke, and I can hear again his voice saying: "Be not ye afraid of them: remember the Lord, who is great and terrible; and fight for your brethren, your sons, your daughters, your wives, and your houses.

*Nehemiah.* How brave they were after that! Though always watchful, always on guard against a sudden attack, I never again saw any of the men overcome by fear.

*Hanani.* No, not even when we worked with a weapon always beside us and with half of the men armed and standing behind us holding our spears, shields and bows, watching lest the enemy surprise us, and listening for the sound of the trumpet which was the call for help.

*Ezra.* But God brought the counsel of our enemies to naught and now at last the work is finished.

*Nehemiah.* And this day we dedicate the wall and thou, Ezra, shalt read the law to us.

[*Nehemiah mounts platform. Trumpet sounds.*

O magnify the Lord with me and let us exalt his name together.

Let us come before his presence with thanksgiving, and make a joyful noise unto him with psalms,

For the Lord is a great God, and a great king above all gods.

Give unto the Lord the glory due unto his name: bring an offering and come into his courts with thanksgiving.

*All.* Praise the Lord, O my soul, and forget not all his benefits.

*Nehemiah.* Ezra shall read to us out of the law.

*Ezra.* [*On platform.*] Hear the word as given by Joshua to your fathers: Take diligent heed to do the commandment and the law, which Moses, the servant of the Lord charged you, to love the Lord your God, and to walk in all his ways, and to keep his commandments, and to cleave unto him, and to serve him with all your hearts and with all your souls.

[*People look serious and bow their heads.*

*Nehemiah.* This day is holy unto the Lord, neither be ye sorry; for the joy of the Lord is your strength. Go forth unto the mount and fetch olive branches, and pine branches and myrtle branches, and branches of thick trees and make for yourselves booths of green that this day may be a festival, a day of pleasure and rejoicing.

*All.* We go, we go.

[*Exeunt, talking and laughing. Ezra, Hanani, Nehemiah remain.*

*Nehemiah.* I can hardly believe that our task is completed. Come with me, I would walk out and view the walls, even as I did on the night of my return. Where then I saw holes, open gateways, broken towers and piles of stones, I shall now see a completed wall, new gates and imposing towers. I would see it with only you two, my faithful friends, as my companions; for through all these long months of hardship and discouragement you have never faltered or grown impatient but have toiled with me to teach this people that

God would never do for them what they could do for themselves; and that only as they used the knowledge they had could he really bless them. Let us depart ere they return.

*[Exeunt.*

**CURTAIN**

# A NEIGHBOR AND HIS WORK

CHARACTERS:
  Merchant.
  Priest.
  Levite.
  Samaritan (*with bundles*).
  Robbers.

## SCENE I

PLACE: *A road through rough, wild country. Chairs and boxes covered with dark material may be used to represent rocks. Ferns, growing plants, etc., add to the effect.*

Merchant. [*Walking back and forth.*] It is good to walk a bit after a long day of riding. The good beast will enjoy the rest, too, as he eats his meal. It was hard to leave the mother and the little ones even for a short time. Yet I must make this journey to buy goods. How eagerly the children will watch for my return. They shall not be disappointed for I will take a gift for each. [*Noise from without. Merchant stops, listens.*] What is that? My beast, has anything happened to him?

[*Starts toward exit. Enter robbers, who run and seize the merchant.*

## A NEIGHBOR AND HIS WORK

*First Robber.* Hold him. Take off his coat.

*Second Robber.* Where is your money, speak!

[*Robbers push man to ground, search him, handle him roughly, take coat, hat, bundles, etc., and depart. After a few seconds man moans, repeats moan.*

[*Enter Priest, chanting, moves slowly across platform, pauses before man.*

*Priest.* Oh, the poor man! Evidently robbers have attacked him. I must hasten. They may be near. [*Looks about with an expression of fear, leaves hurriedly.*

[*Man groans more loudly. Enter Levite, reading as he walks. Man moans.*

*Levite.* [*Looking up from book.*] What is that? [*Sees man.*] Oh, what a looking creature. He must be nearly dead! Well, there is nothing I can do. I can't be burdened with such as he. I have more important things to attend to. He will die anyway. [*Exit.*

[*Man moans, tries to move, falls back.*

*Merchant.* Oh, oh.

*Samaritan.* [*Outside, speaks to animal.*] Well, it's about supper time, isn't it, old friend? You ought not to be very tired. You have had only me to carry to-day, while yesterday you had a heavy load. There now, stand still and eat.

*Merchant.* Help! Help!

[*Enter Samaritan.*

*Samaritan.* Surely I heard a cry for help. [*Sees man.*] Ah. [*Goes to man.*] A poor wounded Jew. [*Takes bandage and bottle from bag, binds wounds, talking to himself meanwhile.*] This is the work of robbers. They have beaten him as well as robbed him. Poor fellow, if I had not come this way he might have died. [*Lifts man on arm, pours liquid through lips.*] There, drink! It will revive you. [*Man opens eyes and looks up.*] Ah, better already? I'll take you with me. My beast is just behind yon rock.

[*Puts man on shoulder and carries him out.*

**CURTAIN**

## SCENE II

PLACE: *In front of house. Keeper in doorway, Samaritan leaving.*

*Samaritan.* I am glad to leave him in such good hands. Take care of him, give him everything he needs. Here is money. [*Gives it to keeper.*] If it is not enough, I will repay thee when next I come.

*Keeper.* What is the man to thee?

*Samaritan.* He is my neighbor.

*Keeper.* Shall we not send word to his friends that he is safe? It will be a long time before he is able to travel.

*Samaritan.* I know them not.

*Keeper.* You know them not? How sayest thou that he is thy neighbor?

*Samaritan.* He was in trouble and needed help and I was the only person to give it. Should I have refused to help him because I knew not his name? I treated him as I should want to be treated. Take good care of him. I will surely return. [*Exit.*

*Keeper.* [*Gazing after him.*] Well, well, a new definition of neighbor. One who needs our help. What a world this would be if we were all neighbors!

**CURTAIN**

# A GIRL WHO KNEW HOW TO BE A FRIEND

CHARACTERS:
  Naomi.
  Ruth.
  Orpha.
  Boaz.
  Overseer.
  Reapers.

## SCENE I

PLACE: *An oriental home.*

*Naomi.* It was but a few years ago that I came to the land of Moab. I came not alone. With me were my husband and my two sons. The famine did not reach us here, and for awhile all went well. My sons found you [*addressing Ruth and Orpha*], the women whom they married. Jehovah blessed us and filled our lives with joy. But how changed is my condition now! The Almighty hath dealt hardly with me, my husband and my sons have been taken away. Now I have heard that there is food in abundance in the homeland. I am going to return, that my last days may be spent among the friends of my youth and in the land that gave me birth.

## A GIRL WHO KNEW HOW TO BE A FRIEND

*Orpha.* Go thou, and we will go with thee, for in the day of thy prosperity and in the day of thy sorrow have we been with thee. Shall we forsake thee now?

*Naomi.* Nay, thou shalt not leave thine own land. Go, return each of you to your mother's home! Jehovah deal kindly with you as ye have dealt with the dead and with me. [*Embraces Ruth and Orpha.*] Go and leave me! I will go my way alone!

*Ruth.* Nay, we will return with thee.

*Naomi.* Why wilt thou go? The hand of Jehovah is gone forth against me. Turn, my daughters. Tarry ye in the land of Moab.

[*Orpha embraces Naomi and leaves her.*

*Naomi.* [*Addressing Ruth.*] Behold, thy sister-in-law hath gone back to her people and to her gods. Return thou after her.

*Ruth.* Entreat me not to leave thee, and to return from following after thee, for whither thou goest I will go, and where thou lodgest I will lodge; thy people shall be my people, and thy God my God; where thou diest, will I die, and there will I be buried. Jehovah do so to me and more also, if aught but death part thee and me.

*Naomi.* Do as seemeth best to thee and may Jehovah reward thee.

[*Exeunt Ruth and Naomi.*

**CURTAIN**

## SCENE II

PLACE: *Field of Boaz.*
*Reapers gleaning in field, singing as they work. Overseer in background. Ruth with reapers.*

*Reaper.* Behold our master, the great Boaz, cometh.
[*Enter Boaz.*
*Boaz.* Jehovah be with thee.
*All.* [*Standing upright.*] Jehovah bless thee.
[*Reapers resume work. Boaz walks about, sees Ruth, watches her.*
*Boaz.* [*Approaching overseer.*] Whose damsel is this?
*Overseer.* It is the Moabitish damsel that came back with Naomi out of the land of Moab. She said, "Let me glean, I pray you, and gather after the reapers among the sheaves"; so she came and hath continued even from the morning until now.
*Boaz.* Let her glean among the sheaves and reproach her not. Also let fall some of the handfuls on purpose for her, and leave them that she may glean them, and rebuke her not.
*Overseer.* It shall be done even as thou sayest.
[*Boaz approaches Ruth.*
*Boaz.* Hearest thou, my daughter. Go not to glean in another field, neither go from hence, but abide here fast by my maidens. Let thine eyes be on the fields that they do reap, and go thou after them, for I have charged the young men that they

shall not touch thee, and when thou art athirst, go unto the vessels and drink of that which the young men have drawn.

*Ruth.* [*Bowing low before Boaz.*] Why have I found grace in thine eyes, that thou shouldst take knowledge of me, seeing I am a stranger?

*Boaz.* It hath fully been showed me, all that thou hast done unto thy mother-in-law since the death of thine husband; and how thou hast left thy father and thy mother and the land of thy nativity, and art come unto a people which thou knewest not heretofore. Jehovah recompense thy work and a full reward be given thee of the Lord God of Israel, under whose wings thou art come to trust.

*Ruth.* Let me find favor in thy sight, my lord, for thou hast comforted me and thou hast spoken friendly unto thine handmaid, though I be not like unto one of thine handmaidens.

*Boaz.* At mealtime come thou hither and eat of the bread and of the corn prepared for the reapers. [*Moves away.*

*Ruth.* He is indeed kind. It is he of whom Naomi hath told me. He is her near kinsman. I wonder—— [*Gazes after Boaz.*] He is her near kinsman.

*Boaz.* [*Soliloquizing.*] And so she is the Moabitess. She is indeed beautiful and kind, I know. Her devotion to Naomi hath proved it,— and I am her near kinsman, the nearest who is free to marry her. It would please Naomi to have me fulfill my obligation. To-morrow I will seek out the women in their home, and offer to marry the damsel and to care for her and Naomi. This will I do, for the Moabitess, Ruth, doth please me. I will fulfill my obligation. Jehovah is my witness.

[*Naomi approaches during Boaz's speech but remains unseen in the background.*]

*Naomi.* Ah, I can see that Ruth hath found favor in the eyes of Boaz. He knoweth the law, that if a man die and leave a wife, his nearest of kin shall marry her. He will fulfill it and Ruth shall be his wife and once more rest shall come to our household. Thanks be unto Jehovah, who hath not left us desolate but hath showed the way to peace. Blessed be His Holy name forever and ever.

CURTAIN

# A THANKSGIVING SERVICE

CHARACTERS:
  Moses.
  Miriam.
  Group of Israelites.

## SCENE I

PLACE: *In the wilderness. Small groups standing talking. Shawls, capes and coats may be worn to cover the white dresses needed in Scene II.*

[*Noise in the distance.*

*First Speaker.* Hark, what is that?
*Second Speaker.* Can it be the Egyptians?
*Chorus.* The Egyptians!
*Third Speaker.* We shall all perish here in the wilderness.
*Fourth Speaker.* Is it for this that we left Egypt?

[*Noise increases.*

*Chorus.* They come! They come!
*Fifth Speaker.* Yes, it is the horses and chariots of Pharaoh.
*Sixth Speaker.* His horsemen and his army.
*Chorus.* We shall all perish!
*Seventh Speaker.* It would have been better to have remained in Egypt than to perish here in the wilderness.

*Eighth Speaker.* Where is Moses?

*Chorus.* Yes, where is Moses?

*Eighth Speaker.* He brought us here. Because there were no graves in Egypt, did he take us away to die in the wilderness? Wherefore hath he dealt thus with us to carry us forth out of Egypt? For it had been better for us to serve the Egyptians than that we should perish here.

*Chorus.* Moses! Moses!

[*Enter Moses.*

*Moses.* Fear not, stand still and see the salvation of Jehovah which he will work for you to-day; for the Egyptians whom ye have seen to-day, ye shall see them again no more forever. Jehovah will fight for you and ye shall hold your peace. [*Silence.*] Hark! I hear a voice. It says: Speak unto the children of Israel that they go forward. Lift thou up thy rod, and stretch out thy hand over the sea, and divide it: and the children of Israel shall go into the midst of the sea on dry ground. And the Egyptians shall know that I am Jehovah, when I have gotten me honor upon Pharaoh, and upon his chariots, and upon his horsemen.

*First Speaker.* We are saved.

*Second Speaker.* Jehovah hath provided a way of escape.

*Chorus.* Praise be unto his holy name.

*Moses.* Come, let us go to the sea and behold the wonders which Jehovah shall perform. Let us go forward, even as he commanded.

[*Exeunt all.*

CURTAIN

## SCENE II

TIME: *The following day, on the other side of Red Sea.*
CHARACTERS *same as in Scene I. Girls in white.*

*First Speaker.* Jehovah did not forget his people.
*Second Speaker.* The Egyptians perished in the sea.
*Third Speaker.* Israel is saved. Great is Jehovah!
*Moses.* He hath remembered us in our need. He hath saved us from the hand of the enemy. Let us give thanks unto him. Let us sing a song of praise.
*Miriam.* [*Coming to front of platform.*] The women of Israel would sing with thee, oh, my brother. Listen unto our song.
*Women.* [*Chant.*]
Sing ye to Jehovah for he hath triumphed gloriously.
The horse and the riders hath he thrown into the sea.
*Miriam.* [*Accompanied by low music of violin, played behind scene.*]
Jehovah is my strength and song
And he is become my salvation.
He is my God, and I will praise Him,
My father's God and I will exalt Him,
Pharaoh's chariots and his host hath he cast into the sea;

And his chosen captains are sunk in the Red Sea.
The deep cover them.
They went down into the depths like a stone.
   *All.* [*Chant.*]
Sing ye to Jehovah for he hath triumphed gloriously.
The horse and the rider hath he thrown into the sea.
   *Miriam.*
Thy right hand, O Jehovah, is glorious in power.
Thy right hand, O Jehovah, dasheth in pieces the enemy.
With the blast of thy nostrils the waters were piled up.
The floods stood upright as a heap;
The deeps were congealed in the heart of the sea.
The enemy said:
"I will pursue, I will overtake, I will divide the spoil."
Thou didst blow with thy wind, the sea covered them.
They sank as lead in the mighty waters.
   *All.* [*Chant.*]
Sing ye to Jehovah for he hath triumphed gloriously.
The horse and the rider hath he thrown into the sea.
   *Miriam.*
Who is like unto thee, O Jehovah, among the gods?
Who is like thee, glorious in holiness!
Fearful in praises, doing wonders!

## A THANKSGIVING SERVICE

Thou in thy loving-kindness hath led the people that thou hath redeemed!
Thou hast guided them in thy strength to thy holy habitation.
Jehovah shall reign forever and ever!
  [*All the girls with Miriam fall to their knees.*
  *Women.*
Jehovah shall reign forever and ever.
  *Moses.* [*Raising his hands toward heaven.*]
Hear our song, O Jehovah, accept the thanks of thy people for their merciful deliverance.
  *Women.*
Jehovah shall reign forever and ever.

CURTAIN

# THE FIRST CHRISTMAS

CHARACTERS:
Three Wise Men.
Mary.
Joseph.
Voice.

## SCENE I

TIME: *Night. Three Wise Men talking together.*

*First Wise Man.* Think you that we shall see the star to-night?

*Second Wise Man.* It is time for it to appear. Long have we watched and waited for its coming.

*Third Wise Man.* Never were the stars so bright as to-night. Look at that large one in the east. Is it not different from others.

> [*All look. If desired, a star may be represented by placing an electric light under a paper star.*

*First Wise Man.* Its radiance is unlike that of the other stars.

*Second Wise Man.* It is moving.

*Third Wise Man.* Can it be the Star that is to herald the birth of the king?

*Second Wise Man.* It is written, and thou Bethlehem, in the land of Judah, art not least among the princes of Judah: for out of thee shall come a governor that shall rule my people Israel. The Star certainly moves. Let us follow it.

*First Wise Man.* Let us seek the king.

*Second and Third Wise Man.* Yes, let us seek the king. [*Exeunt all.*

**CURTAIN**

## SCENE II

PLACE: *A stable, with door ajar.*

[*Enter Three Wise Men.*

*First Wise Man.* Can this be the place?

*Second Wise Man.* It was strange that Herod did not know where the king was to be born.

*Third Wise Man.* He could only send us to Bethlehem, and that he knew because it was told by the prophets.

*Second Wise Man.* Surely the star has ceased to move and is shining on yon building.

*First and Third Wise Men.* It is! It is!

[*Singing in the distance. Any appropriate Christmas hymn.*

*First Wise Man.* Let us enter.

[*All go into building. Through the open door may be seen in the far corner of the room, a manger, from which a light is shining. Standing near are Joseph and Mary.*

*First Wise Man.* Where is he that is born King of the Jews, for we have seen his star in the east, and are come to worship him.

*Joseph.* Come near and behold him.

[*Men approach manger, fall on knees.*

*Mary.*
My soul doth magnify the Lord,
And my spirit hath rejoiced in God my Saviour.
For he hath looked upon the low estate of his handsmaid.
For behold, from henceforth all generations shall call me blessed.

[*Wise Men rise and present gifts to Mary and Joseph.*

*Second Wise Man.* We would make a gift unto our king. We have each brought our best.

*First Wise man.* I bring gold.

*Second Wise Man.* I bring frankincense.

*Third Wise Man.* And I bring myrrh.

*Joseph.* For all your gifts the king will have need.

[*As wise men reach the entrance of room, they pause and look toward the manger.*

*First Wise Man.* The holy child! Long shall this night be remembered.

[*Wise men outside the stable.*

*First Wise Man.* It is indeed the king.

*Second Wise Man.* Didst thou feel the presence of the angels as we knelt before the child?

*Third Wise Man.* Our gifts seemed so small even though we brought our best.

*Second Wise Man.* Our search has been rewarded. We have seen the young child and his mother.

*Third Wise Man.* He is indeed the Messiah.

Who could behold the beauty of that face, see the heavenly light, feel the presence of the angels and be guided by the Star and fail to believe?

*First Wise Man.* Let us hasten and tell Herod where the child may be found.

*Second Wise Man.* Must we return to him? He did not seem pleased at the news we brought.

*First Wise Man.* Not at first, but later he said, Go and search diligently for the young child; and when ye have found him bring me word again, that I may come and worship him also.

*Second Wise Man.* I know he said that but I could not believe him sincere. I think he means harm to the child. He fears a new king. I think we should return another way.

*First Wise Man.* Will not Herod be angry?

[*Sound of mother crooning a lullaby. Men fall to knees in attitude of adoration and so remain during singing.*

*Voice.* Glory to God in the highest, and on earth peace, good will to men.

[*After a moment of silence the three men rise.*

*First Wise Man.* As I knelt a voice seemed to speak to me and say, Return by another way.

*Second Wise Man.* It spoke also to me.

*Third Wise Man.* And to me.

*First Wise Man.* Let us be going then. We have seen and worshipped our King. He has our first allegiance.

*Third Wise Man.* Glory to God in the Highest.

*Second Wise Man.* And on earth peace.

*First Wise Man.* Good will to men.

[*Exeunt all.*
[*A Christmas hymn sung from a distance makes a very fitting close.*]

CURTAIN

Printed in the United States
58809LVS00004B/124